JOHN PRINE
for Ukulele

Photo by Michael Ochs Archives / Getty Images

ISBN 978-1-70510-405-7

Visit Hal Leonard Online at
www.halleonard.com

Contact us:
Hal Leonard
7777 West Bluemound Road
Milwaukee, WI 53213
Email: info@halleonard.com

In Europe, contact:
Hal Leonard Europe Limited
42 Wigmore Street
Marylebone, London, W1U 2RN
Email: info@halleonardeurope.com

In Australia, contact:
Hal Leonard Australia Pty. Ltd.
4 Lentara Court
Cheltenham, Victoria, 3192 Australia
Email: info@halleonard.com.au

Angels from Montgomery

Words and Music by John Prine

this old house — would have burnt — down a long —

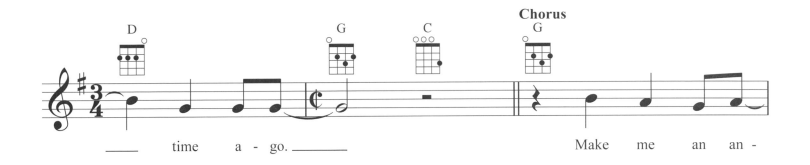

Chorus

— time a - go. — Make me an an -

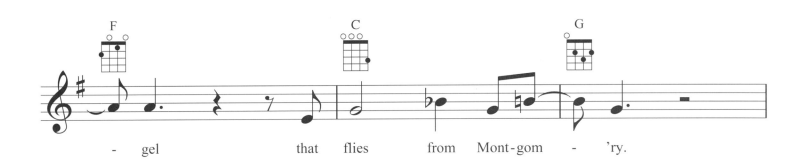

- gel that flies from Mont-gom - 'ry.

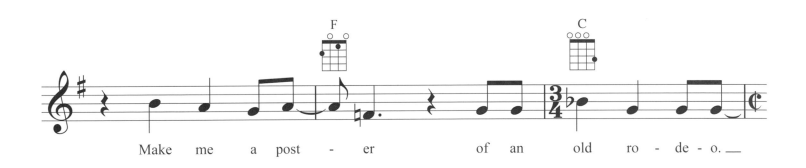

Make me a post - er of an old ro - de - o. —

— Just give me one — thing that

Additional Lyrics

2. When I was a young girl, well, I had me a cowboy.
   He weren't much to look at, just a free rambling man.
   But that was a long time, and no matter how I try,
   The years just flow by like a broken-down dam.

3. There's flies in the kitchen; I can hear 'em there, buzzing.
   And I ain't done nothing since I woke up today.
   How the hell can a person go to work in the morning
   And come home in the evening and have nothing to say?

Clay Pigeons

Words and Music by Michael Fuller

First note

1., 4. I'm go-ing down ___ to the Grey-hound sta-

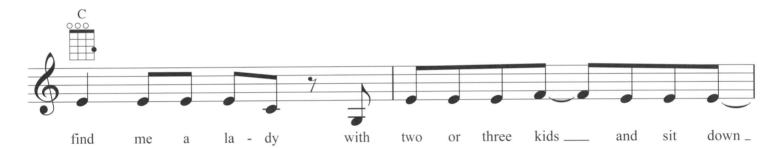

tion, gon-na buy a tick-et to ride. ___ I'm gon-na

find me a la-dy with two or three kids ___ and sit down ___

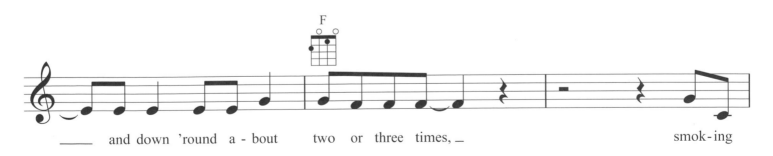

___ by her side. ___ We'll ride till the sun comes up ___

___ and down 'round a-bout two or three times, ___ smok-ing

cig - a - rettes   in ____ the   last   seat;   { sing   this
                                                       { sing   my

song   for   the   peo - ple   I   meet,   and   get   a -
song   for   the   peo - ple   I   meet,   and   get   a -

long with   it   all, ___   where the   peo - ple   say   "y'all."
long with   it   all, ___   where the   peo - ple   say   "y'all."

I'll   sing   a   song   with   a   friend, ___
Feed   the   pi - geons   some   clay, ____

change   the   shape   that   I'm   in, _____
turn   the   night   in - to   day, ____

and   get   back   in   the   game, ___   and   start
and   start   talk - ing   a - gain ____   when   I

play - ing a - gain. ___
know what to say. ___

Verse

2. I'd like to stay, ___ but I might have to go, ___ to start

o - ver a - gain. __ I might go back down to Tex - as, or

go to some - where _ that I _____ nev - er been; _ and get

up in the morn - ing, and go out at night, __ and I won't

have to go home. ___ Get used to

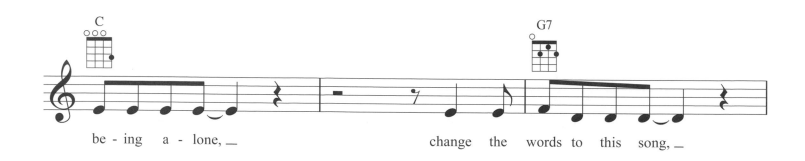

be - ing a - lone, ___ change the words to this song, ___

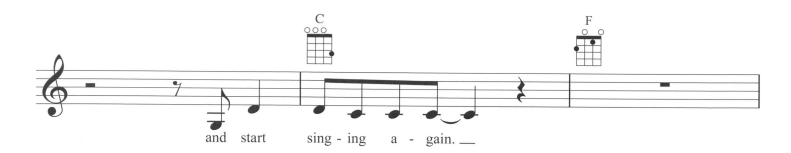

and start sing - ing a - gain. ___

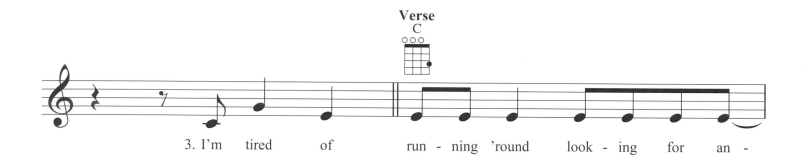

Verse

3. I'm tired of run - ning 'round look - ing for an -

- swers to ques - tions that I al - read - y know. ___

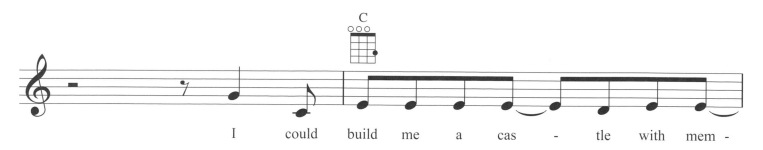

I could build me a cas - tle with mem -

-'ries,   just to have some-where to go. ____   Count the

days   and   the nights ____ that it takes to get back ____   in the

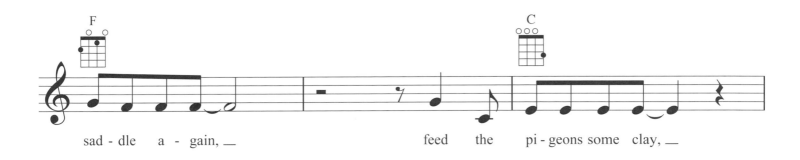

sad - dle a - gain, ____   feed   the   pi - geons some clay, __

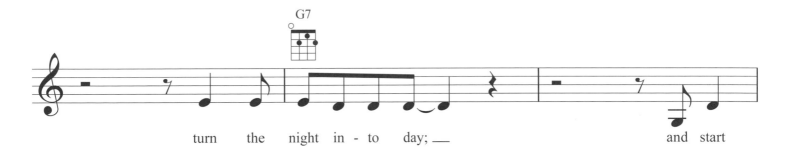

turn   the night in - to day; ____   and start

talk - ing a - gain ____ when   I   know what to   say. ____

Coda

D.C. al Coda

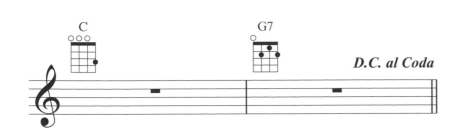

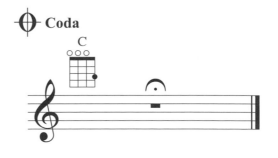

Crazy as a Loon

Words and Music by John E. Prine and Pat McLaughlin

First note

Moderately
N.C.

%. Verse

1. Back be - fore I was a mov - ie star,
(2.) Nash - ville
(3.) sav - vy,

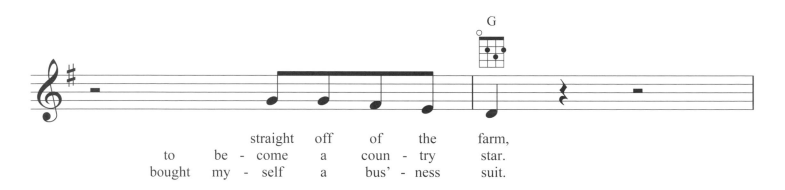

straight off of the farm,
to be - come a coun - try star.
bought my - self a bus' - ness suit.

I had a pic - ture of an - oth - er man's wife _____
Ev - 'ry night you'd find me hang - in' _____
I head - ed up to New York Cit - y, _____

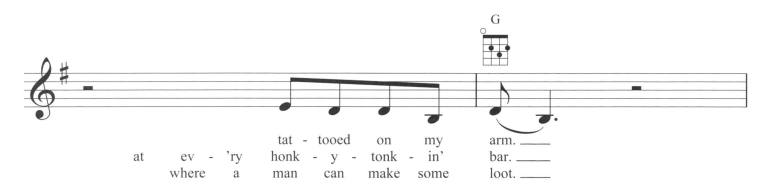

tat - tooed on my arm. _____
at ev - 'ry honk - y - tonk - in' bar. _____
where a man can make some loot. _____

You'll be walk - ing 'round in cir - cles
You'll be walk - ing 'round in cir - cles

down on Hol - ly - wood and Vine. ___
look - ing for that coun - try rhyme. ___

You'll be wait - ing on a phone call

at the wrong ___ end of a broom.

Yes, that town - 'll make you cra - zy,

1.

cra - zy as a loon. ___

So I head-ed down to loon. ____

D.S. al Coda

So I gath-ered up my loon.

Coda

Outro-Chorus

So I'm up here in the north woods,

just star-ing at a lake,

won-d'ring just ex-act-ly how ____ much

they think a man can take. ____

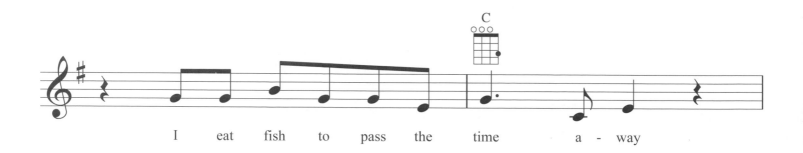

I eat fish to pass the time a - way

'neath this blue Ca - na - di - an moon.

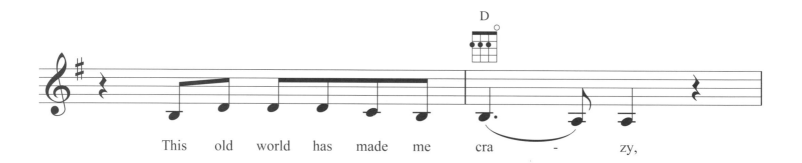

This old world has made me cra - zy,

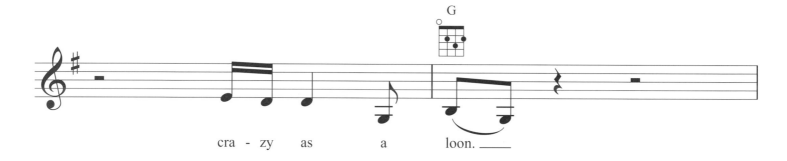

cra - zy as a loon. ___

Oh, lord, this world will make you cra - zy,

cra - zy as a loon. ___

Fish and Whistle

Words and Music by John E. Prine

First note

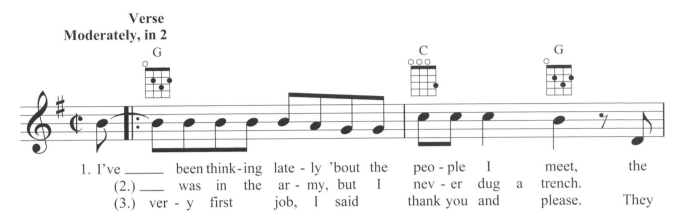

Verse
Moderately, in 2

1. I've _____ been think-ing late-ly 'bout the peo-ple I meet, the
(2.) ____ was in the ar-my, but I nev-er dug a trench. The
(3.) ver-y first job, I said thank you and please. They

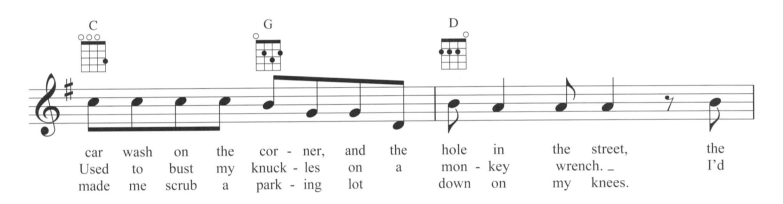

car wash on the cor-ner, and the hole in the street, the
Used to bust my knuck-les on a mon-key wrench. ___ I'd
made me scrub a park-ing lot down on my knees.

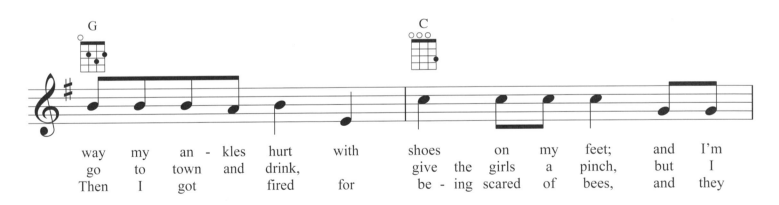

way my an-kles hurt with shoes on my feet; and I'm
go to town and drink, give the girls a pinch, but I
Then I got fired for be-ing scared of bees, and they

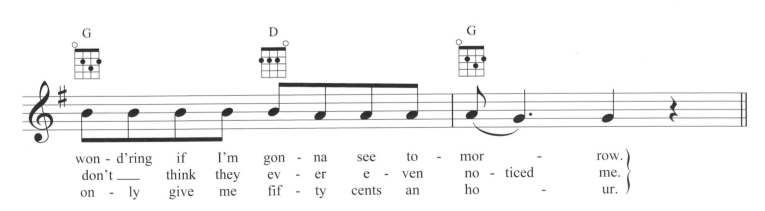

won-d'ring if I'm gon-na see to-mor - - row.
don't ___ think they ev - er e-ven no-ticed me.
on-ly give me fif-ty cents an ho - ur.

Chorus

Fa - ther, for - give __ us for what we must do. You for - give us, we'll __

__ for - give you. We'll __ for - give each oth - er till we

both turn blue, then we'll whis - tle and go fish - ing in

1. heav - en.

2., 3. 2. I __ heav - en.

Bridge

Fish and whis - tle, whis - tle and fish. Eat ev - 'ry - thing that they

put on your dish. And when we get through, we'll make a big wish that we

Hello in There

Words and Music by John Prine

First note

Verse
Moderately slow, in 2

1. We had an a - part - ment in the cit - y.
3. Me and Lor - et - ta, we don't talk much more.

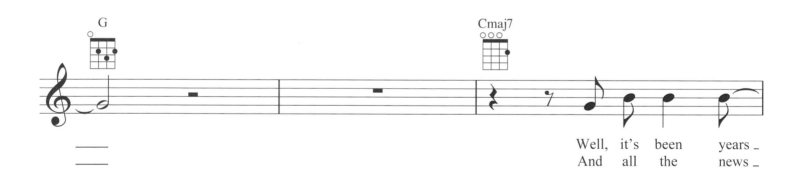

Me and Lor - et - ta liked ____ liv - ing there. ____
She sits and stares through the ____ back door screen. _

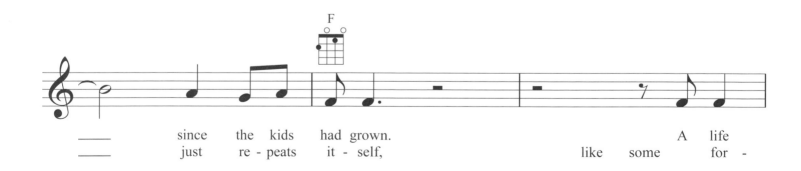

____ Well, it's been years ____
____ And all the news _

____ since the kids had grown. A life
____ just re - peats it - self, like some for -

of their own, ___ | left us _____ a - lone.
got - ten dream __ | that we've ___ both seen.

Verse

2. John and Lin - da live in O -
4. Some-day I'll go _____ and call up Ru -

- ma - ha, and Joe is some -
- dy; ___ we worked to - geth -

- where on the road.
- er at the fac - to - ry.

We lost Da - vy in the Ko - re - an War,
But what could I _____ say if he asks, ___ "What's new?"

and I still don't know what for. ___ Don't mat - ter an -
"Noth - ing. What's with you?" __ "Noth - ing much __

Outro-Verse

lo."   So, if you're walk-

ing   down the street ____ some - time

and spot some hol - low, _____ an - cient eyes, ____

please don't   just   pass 'em   by ___

____ and stare   as if you did - n't care. ___

Say, "Hel - lo in there, _____ hel - lo."

In Spite of Ourselves

Words and Music by John E. Prine

First note

Verse
Moderately

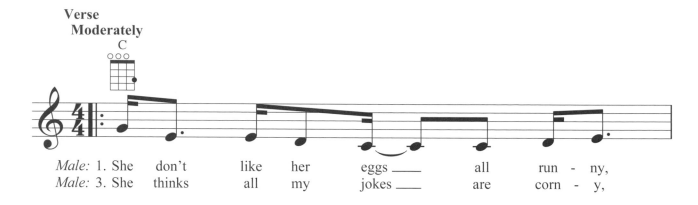

Male: 1. She don't like her eggs ____ all run - ny,
Male: 3. She thinks all my jokes ____ are corn - y,

she thinks cross - ing her legs ____ is fun - ny.
con - vict mov - ies make ____ her horn - y,

She looks down her nose ____ at mon - ey, she
She likes ketch - up on her scram - bled eggs, ____

gets it on ____ like the Eas - ter Bun - ny.
swears like a sail - or when she shaves her legs. ____ She

She's my ba - by, I'm _____ her hon - ey. I'm
takes a lick - ing and keeps on tick - ing. I'm

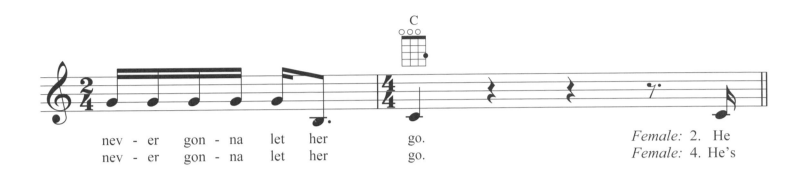

nev - er gon - na let her go.
nev - er gon - na let her go.

Female: 2. He
Female: 4. He's

Verse

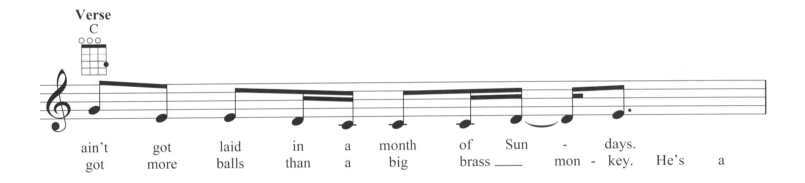

ain't got laid in a month of Sun - days.
got more balls than a big brass _____ mon - key. He's a

Caught him once _____ and he was sniff - ing my un - dies. He
whacked - out weird - o and a love - bug junk - ie.

ain't too sharp, but he gets things done,
Sly as a fox, cra - zy as a loon,

23

drinks his beer _____ like it's ox - y - gen. _____
pay - day comes _____ and he's a - howl - ing at the moon.

He's my ba - by and I'm his hon - ey. I'm
He's my ba - by, I don't mean may - be. I'm

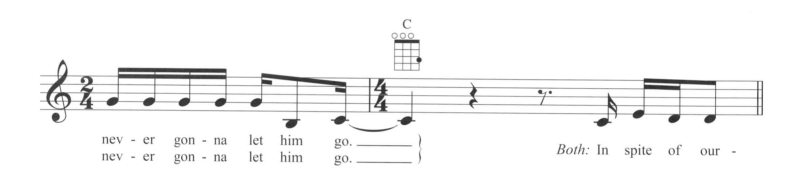

nev - er gon - na let him go. _____ }
nev - er gon - na let him go. _____ }

Both: In spite of our -

𝄋 Chorus

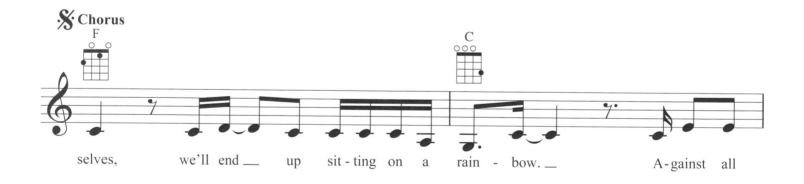

selves, we'll end __ up sit - ting on a rain - bow. __ A - gainst all

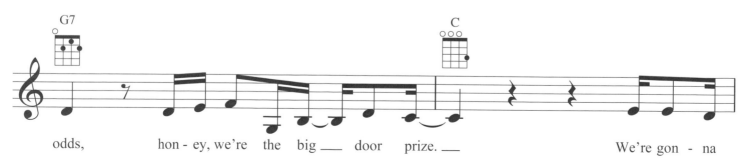

odds, hon - ey, we're the big __ door prize. __ We're gon - na

24

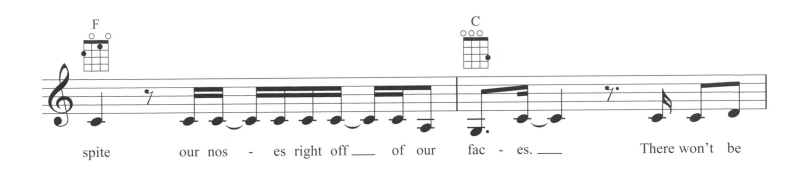

spite   our   nos - es   right off ___ of   our   fac - es. ___   There won't be

To Coda ⊕ | 1.

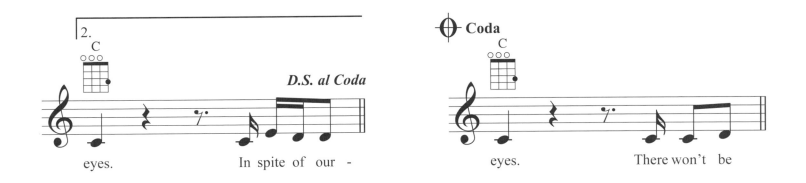

noth - ing   but   big   old   hearts _   danc - ing   in   our   eyes.

| 2.

⊕ **Coda**

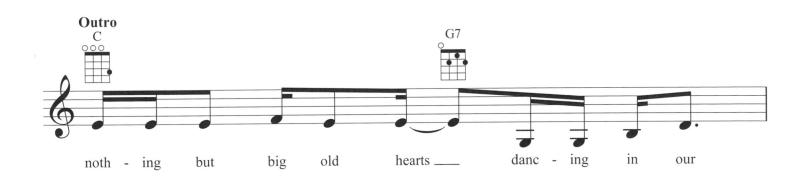

eyes.   **D.S. al Coda**

eyes.   There won't be

In spite of our -

Outro

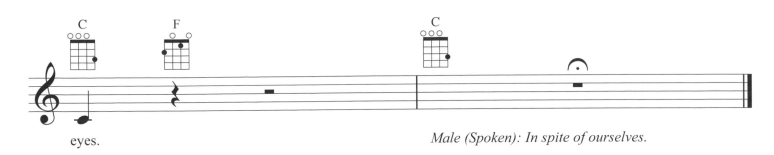

noth - ing   but   big   old   hearts ____   danc - ing   in   our

eyes.

Male (Spoken): In spite of ourselves.

Long Monday

Words and Music by John E. Prine and Keith Sykes

First note

Verse
Moderately, in 2

1. You and me, ____ sit-ting in the back of my
2. We made love ____ in ev-'ry way ____ love _____
3. Soul to soul, ____ heart ____ to heart, _____ and

mem - o - ry ____
can be made. _
cheek to cheek. _

like a hon-ey bee ____
And we made time: ____
Now come on, ba - by,

buz - zing 'round a glass of sweet ____ Cha - blis.
looked like ____ time ____ could ____ nev - er fade.
give me a kiss ____ that - 'll last all week.

A ra - di - o's on, ____ win-dow's rolled up, and my
Fri - day night ____ we both ____ made ____ the
The thought _ of you ____ leav - ing a - gain ____

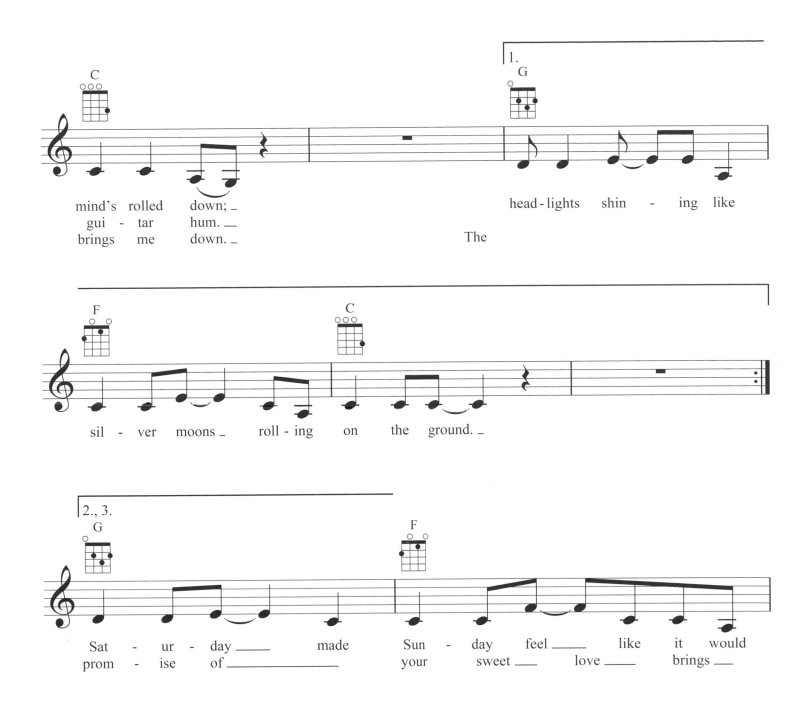

mind's rolled down; _   head-lights shin - ing like
gui - tar hum. _
brings me down. _   The

sil - ver moons _ roll - ing on the ground. _

Sat - ur - day _____ made Sun - day feel _____ like it would
prom - ise of _____ your sweet _____ love _____ brings _____

nev - er come. _____ ⎫
me a - round. _____ ⎬   Gon - na be a long _____

Chorus

_____ Mon - day,   sit - ting all a - lone on a

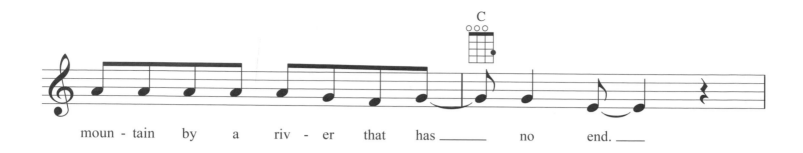

moun - tain by a riv - er that has _____ no end. _____

Gon-na be a long _____ Mon - day,

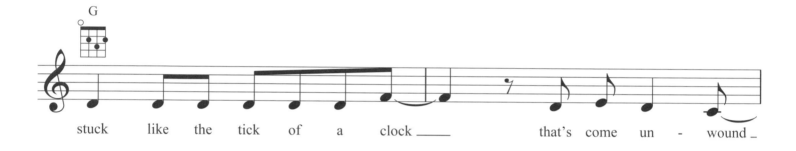

stuck like the tick of a clock _____ that's come un - wound _

_____ a - gain. _____

D.C. al Coda
(take 2nd ending)

Coda

a - gain _____

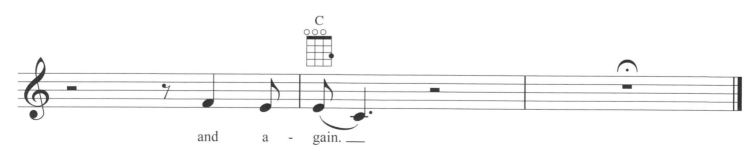

and a - gain. _____

28

Illegal Smile

Words and Music by John Prine

First note

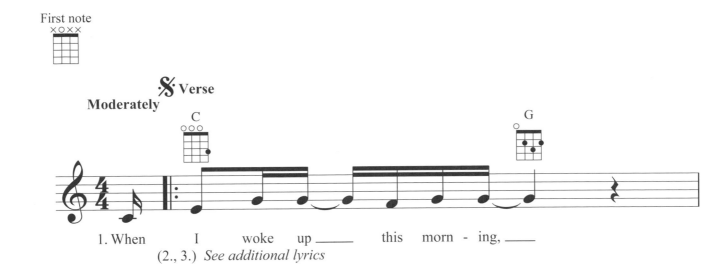

Moderately *Verse*

1. When I woke up _____ this morn-ing, _____
(2., 3.) *See additional lyrics*

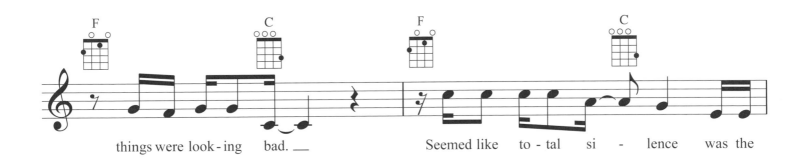

things were look-ing bad. _____ Seemed like to-tal si - lence was the

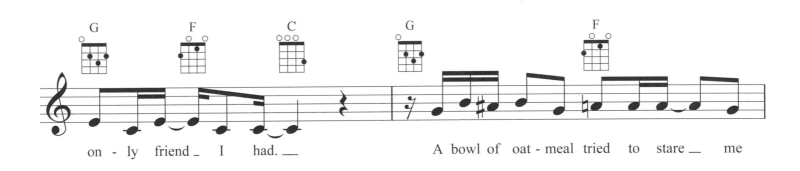

on - ly friend _ I had. _____ A bowl of oat-meal tried to stare _ me

down, and won. And it was twelve o' - clock _ be-fore I re-al-ized I was hav-

Pre-Chorus
Freely

- ing no fun. Ah, but for - tu - nate - ly, ___ I have the key ___ to es -

Chorus
Moderate Waltz

cape re - al - i - ty. ___ And you may see me to -

night with an il - le - gal smile. It don't

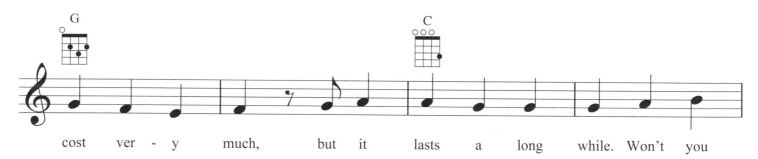

cost ver - y much, but it lasts a long while. Won't you

please tell the man I did - n't kill an - y -

To Coda ⊕

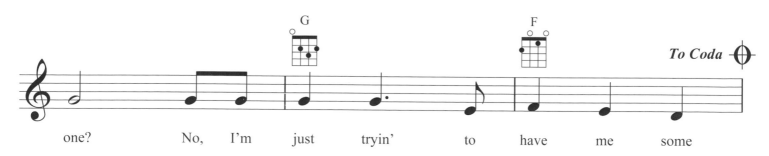

one? No, I'm just tryin' to have me some

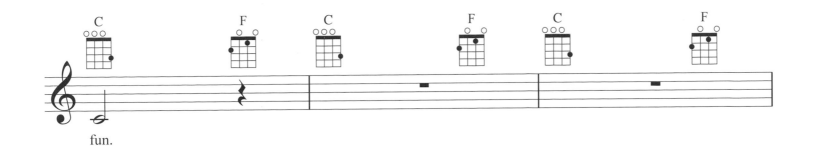

fun.

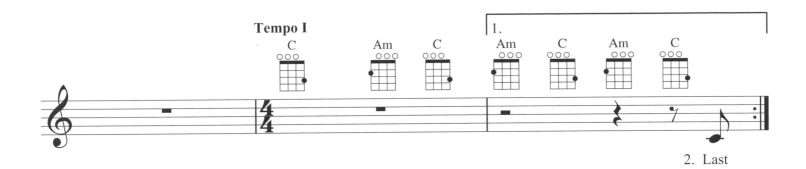

Tempo I

2. Last

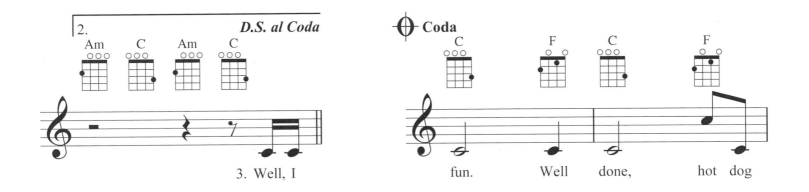

D.S. al Coda

⊕ **Coda**

3. Well, I

fun.   Well   done,   hot dog

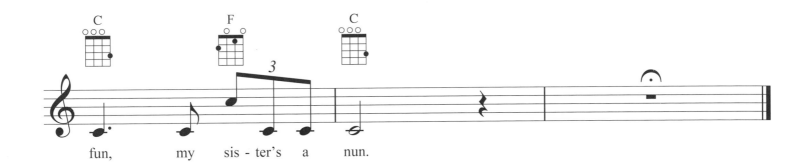

fun,   my   sis - ter's   a   nun.

Additional Lyrics

2. Last time I checked my bankroll, it was getting thin.
   Sometimes it seems like the bottom is the only place I've been.
   I chased a rainbow down a one-way street: dead end.
   And all my friends turned out to be insurance salesmen.

3. Well, I sat down in my closet with all my overalls,
   Tryin' to get away from all the ears inside my walls.
   I dreamed the police heard everything I thought; what then?
   Well, I went to court and the judge's name was Hoffman.

Paradise

Words and Music by John Prine

First note

Verse
Moderately, in 1

1. When I was a child, my fam-'ly would
(2.–4.) *See additional lyrics*

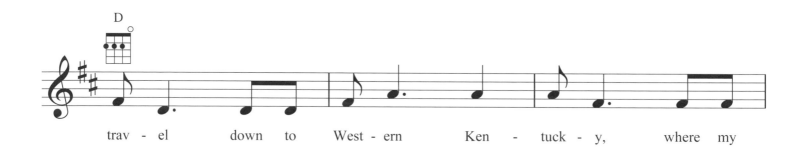

trav-el down to West-ern Ken-tuck-y, where my

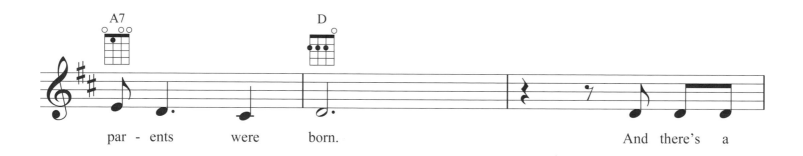

par-ents were born. And there's a

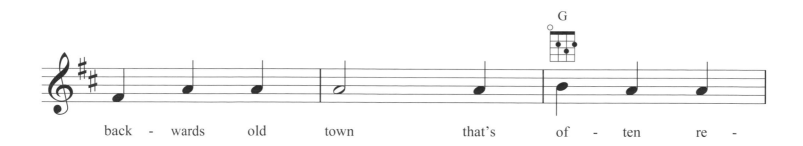

back-wards old town that's of-ten re-

mem - bered _____ so man - y _____ times that my

Chorus

mem - 'ries are worn. And, "Dad - dy, won't you

take me back to Muhl - en - berg ___ Coun - ty, down

by the Green ___ Riv - er, where Par - a - dise

lay?" "Well, I'm sor - ry, my _____

son, but you're too late in ask - ing.

Mis - ter   Pea - bod - y's   coal   train   has

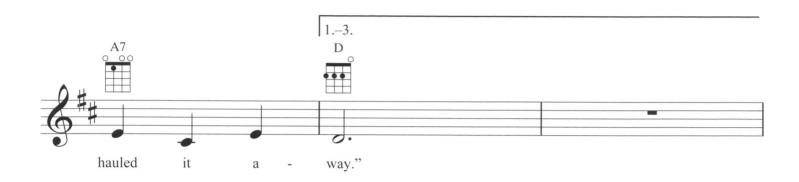

hauled   it   a - way."

2. Well,   way."
3. Then   the
4. When   I

Additional Lyrics

2. Well, sometimes we'd travel right down the Green River
   To the abandoned old prison down by Airdrie Hill,
   Where the air smelled like snakes, and we'd shoot with our pistols,
   But empty pop bottles was all we would kill.

3. Then the coal company came with the world's largest shovel,
   And they tortured the timber and stripped all the land.
   Well, they dug for their coal till the land was forsaken,
   Then they wrote it all down as the progress of man.

4. When I die, let my ashes float down the Green River.
   Let my soul roll on up to the Rochester Dam.
   I'll be halfway to Heaven, with Paradise waiting
   Just five miles away from wherever I am.

Sam Stone

Words and Music by John Prine

First note

Verse

Moderately

1. Sam Stone came home to his wife and fam - i -
   (2., 3.) *See additional lyrics*

ly af - ter serv - ing in ___ the con - flict o - ver - seas. ___

___ And the time that he served ___ had

shat - tered all his nerves, ___ and left a lit - tle shrap -

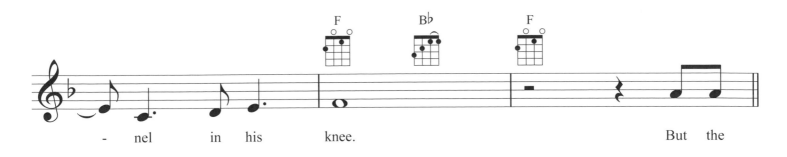

- nel in his knee. But the

Additional Lyrics

2. Sam Stone's welcome home didn't last too long.
   He went to work when he'd spent his last dime.
   And Sammy took to stealing when he got that empty feeling
   For a hundred-dollar habit without overtime.

Pre-Chorus 2: And the gold ran through his veins like a thousand railroad trains,
   And eased his mind in the hours that he chose,
   While the kids ran around wearing other people's clothes.

3. Sam Stone was alone when he popped his last balloon,
   Climbing walls while sitting in a chair.
   Well, he played his last request while the room smelled just like death,
   With an overdose hovering in the air.

Pre-Chorus 3: But life had lost its fun and there was nothing to be done
   But trade his house that he bought on the G.I. Bill
   For a flag-draped casket on a local heroes' hill.

Spanish Pipedream

Words and Music by John Prine and Jeff Kent

First note

1. She was a lev-el-head-ed danc-er _____ on the
(2.) sat there at the ta-ble _____ and I

road to al-co-hol, _____ and I was just a sol-
act-ed real na-ive, _____ for I knew that top-less la-

-dier _____ on my way to Mon-tre-al. _____ Well, she
-dy _____ had ___ some-thing up ___ her sleeve. ___ Well, she

pressed her chest ___ a-gainst ___ me a-bout the time the juke-box broke. ___
danced a-round ___ the bar-room and she did the hootch-y coo. ___

Yeah, she gave me a peck __ on the back of my neck, __ and
Yeah, she sang her __ song __ all night __ long, __

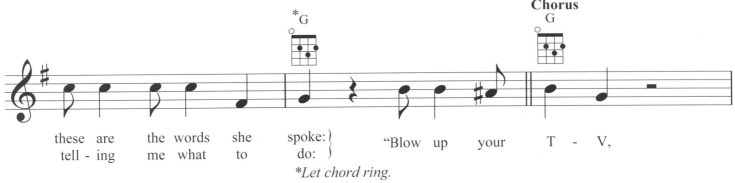

Chorus

these are the words she spoke:} "Blow up your T - V,
tell - ing me what to do: }
Let chord ring.

throw a - way your pa - per, go to the

coun - try, build you a home.

Plant a lit - tle gar - den, eat a lot of

peach - es. Try and find Je - sus

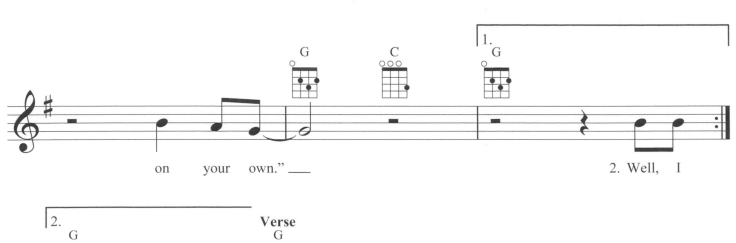

on   your   own." ___   2. Well,   I

Verse

3. Well,   I   was   young _   and   hun - gry,   and   a -

bout   to   leave _   that   place, ___   when   just   as   I ___   was   leav-

- ing,   well,   she   looked   me   in ___   the   face. ___   I   said,

"You must   know _   the   an - swer."   She   said,   "No,   but   I'll give   it   a   try." _

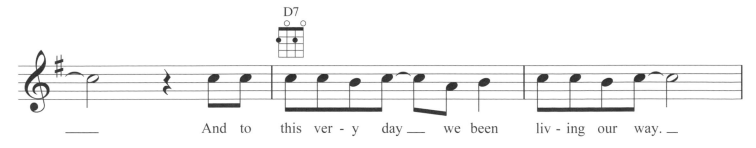

___   And   to   this   ver - y   day _   we   been   liv - ing   our   way. _

*Let chord ring.

Here is the rea - son why: We blew up our T - V,

threw a - way our pa - per, went to the

coun - try, built us a home.

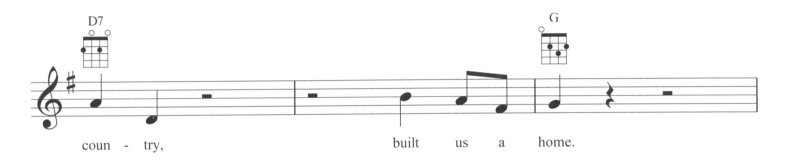

Had a lot of chil - dren, fed 'em on ____

peach - es. They all found Je - sus

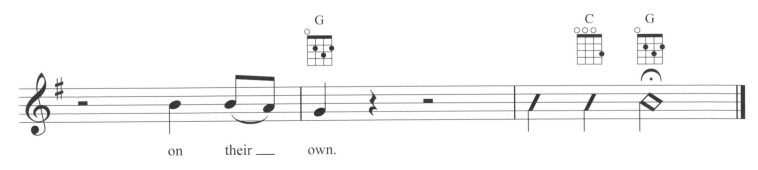

on their ____ own.

Outro-Chorus

Summer's End

Words and Music by John E. Prine and Pat McLaughlin

First note

Verse
Moderately, in 2

1. Sum-mer's end's __ a - round the bend, __ just
(2.) nev - er know __ how far from home __ you're
3. Val - en - tines __ break hearts and minds __ at

fly - ing. __ The swim-ming suits __ are
feel - ing __ un - til you've watched _ the
ran - dom. __ That old Eas - ter egg __ ain't

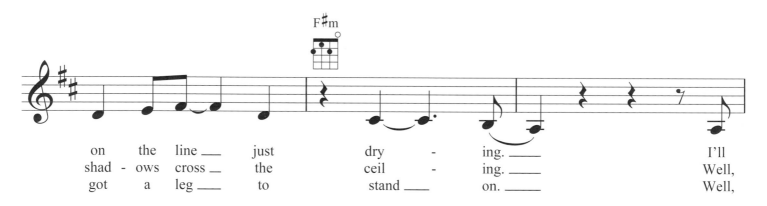

on the line __ just dry - ing. __ I'll
shad - ows cross __ the ceil - ing. __ Well,
got a leg __ to stand __ on. __ Well,

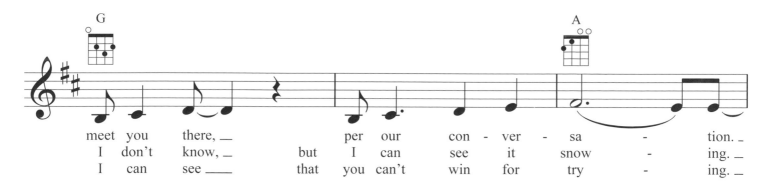

meet you there, __ per our con - ver - sa - tion. __
I don't know, __ but I can see it snow - ing. __
I can see __ that you can't win for try - ing. __

44

_____ we thought ___ was haunt - ed,

Sum-mer's end ___ came fast - er than ___ we want -

Chorus

ed. Come on home. _____ Come on home. _

_____ No, you don't have ___ to

1.

be a - lone. ____ Come on home. _

2.

Just come on home. ___

45

Sweet Revenge

Words and Music by John Prine

First note

Verse
Moderate Blues-Rock

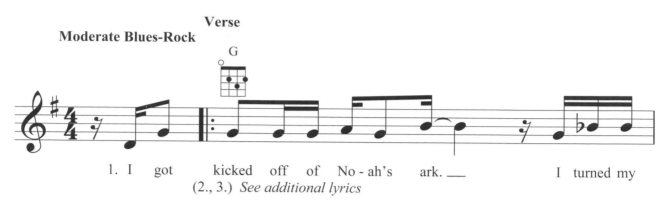

1. I got kicked off of No-ah's ark. ___ I turned my
(2., 3.) *See additional lyrics*

cheek to un-kind re-marks. _ There was two of ev-er-y-thing, _ but one of

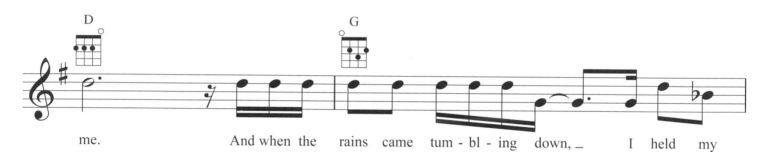

me. And when the rains came tum-bl-ing down, _ I held my

breath and I stood my ground, and I watched that ship go sail-ing out to

Chorus

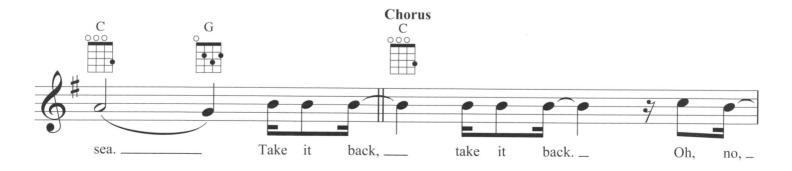

sea. _____ Take it back, ___ take it back. _ Oh, no, _

Additional Lyrics

2. I caught an aisle seat on a plane, drove an English teacher half insane,
   Making up jokes about bicycle spokes and red balloons.
   So I called up my local DJ, and he didn't have a lot to say,
   But the radio has learned all of my favorite tunes.

3. The white meat is on the run, and the dark meat is far too done,
   And the milkman left me a note yesterday:
   "Get out of this town by noon! You're coming on way too soon.
   And besides that, we never liked you anyway."

That's the Way the World Goes 'Round

Words and Music by John E. Prine

First note

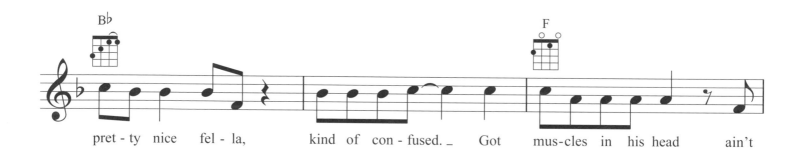

1. I know a guy ___ that's got a lot to lose. ___ He's a

pret - ty nice fel - la, kind of con - fused. _ Got mus-cles in his head ain't

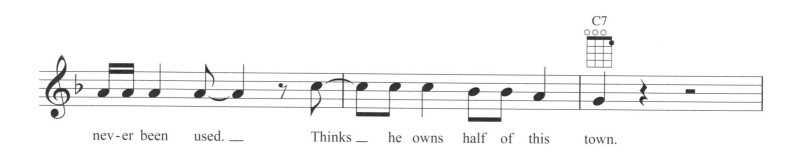

nev-er been used. _ Thinks _ he owns half of this town.

Starts ___ drink-ing heav-y, gets a big red nose, ___

beats his old la-dy with a rub-ber hose. __ Then he takes her out to din-ner, buys __

____ her new clothes. That's the way __ that the world goes 'round.

𝄋 Chorus

That's the way __ that the world goes 'round. You're up one day, __ the

next you're down. __ It's a half an inch of wa-ter and you think you're gon-na drown.

To Coda ⊕

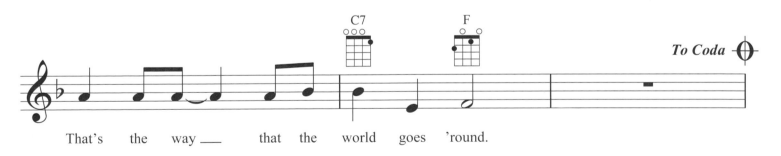

That's the way __ that the world goes 'round.

Verse

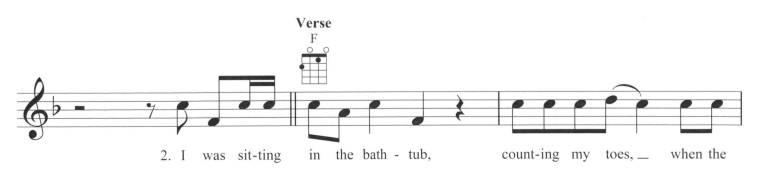

2. I was sit-ting in the bath-tub, count-ing my toes, __ when the

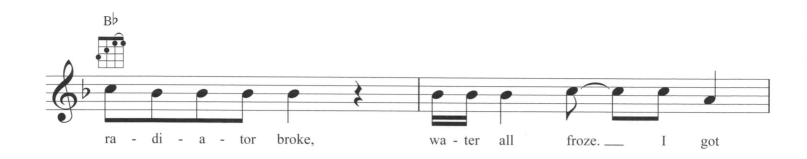

ra - di - a - tor broke, wa - ter all froze. ___ I got

stuck in the ice ___ with - out my clothes, _ na - ked as the eyes of a

clown. I was cry - ing ice ___ cubes,

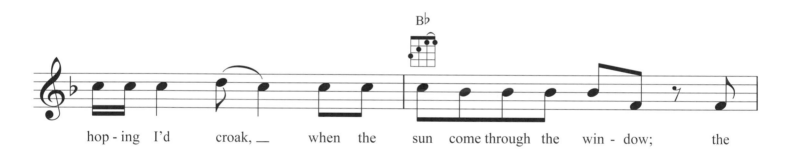

hop - ing I'd croak, ___ when the sun come through the win - dow; the

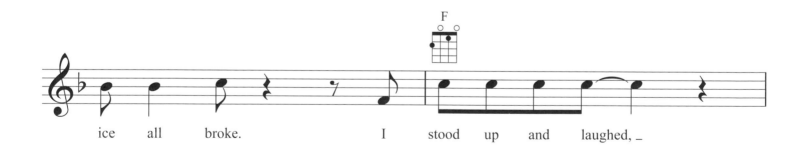

ice all broke. I stood up and laughed, _

D.S. al Coda

thought it was a joke. _ That's the way ___ that the world goes 'round.

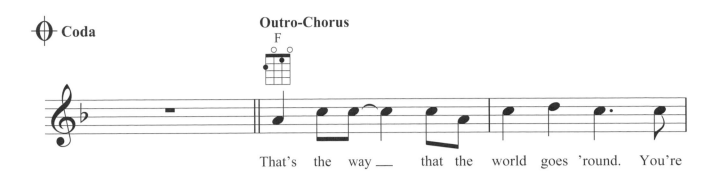

That's the way __ that the world goes 'round. You're

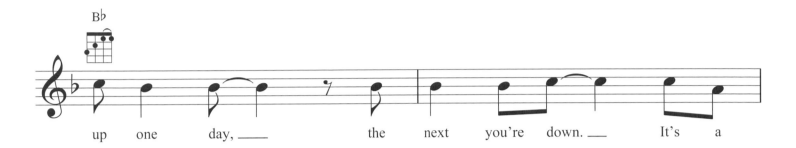

up one day, ____ the next you're down. __ It's a

half an inch of wa - ter and you think you're gon - na drown.

That's the way __ that the world goes 'round. That's the way __ that the

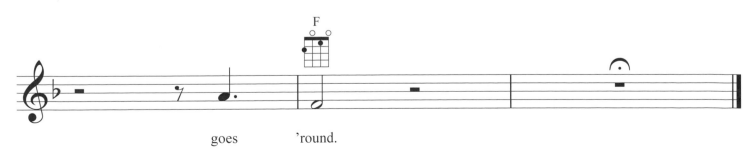

world goes 'round. That's the way __ that the world __

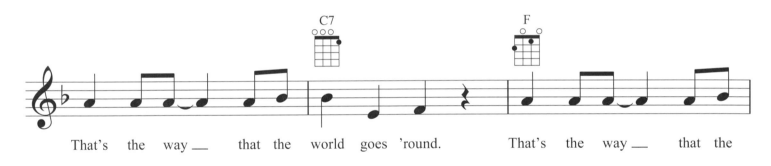

goes 'round.

When I Get to Heaven

Words and Music by John E. Prine

First note

Intro
Slowly, very freely

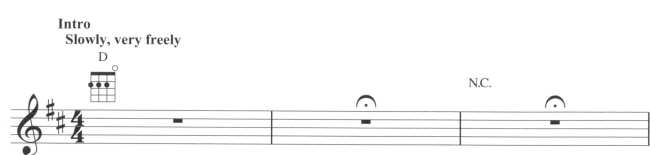

*(Spoken:) When I get to heaven, I'm gonna shake God's hand,
thank Him for more blessings than one man can stand.
Then I'm gonna get a guitar and start a rock 'n' roll band,
check into a swell hotel. Ain't the afterlife grand?*

Moderately bright, in 2   **Chorus**

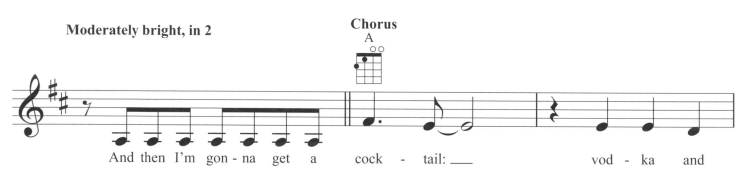

And then I'm gon-na get a cock-tail: ___ vod-ka and

gin-ger ale. ___ Yeah, I'm gon-na smoke a cig-a-rette ___ that's

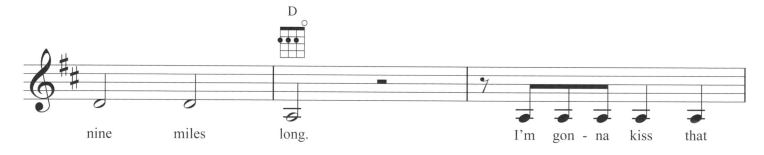

nine miles long. I'm gon-na kiss that

pret-ty girl ___ on the tilt-a-whirl. ___

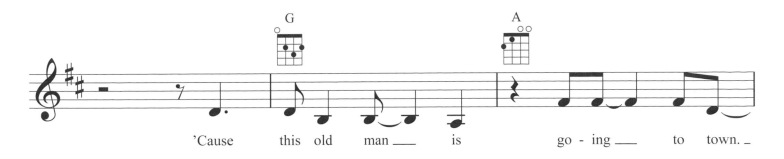

'Cause this old man ___ is go - ing ___ to town. ⌐

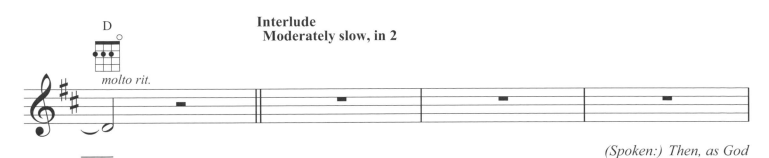

Interlude
Moderately slow, in 2

molto rit.

(Spoken:) Then, as God

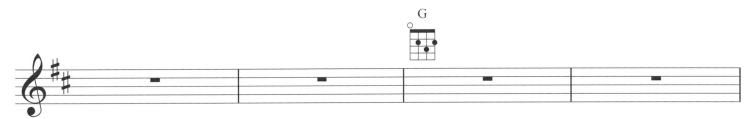

is my witness,   I'm getting back into show business.   I'm gonna open up a

nightclub called "The Tree of Forgiveness,"   and forgive everybody ever done me any harm.

Why, I might even invite a few choice critics.   Those

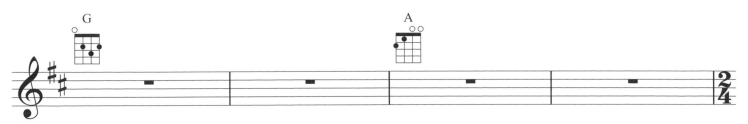

syphilitic parasitics.   Buy 'em a pint of Smithwick's and smother 'em with my charm.

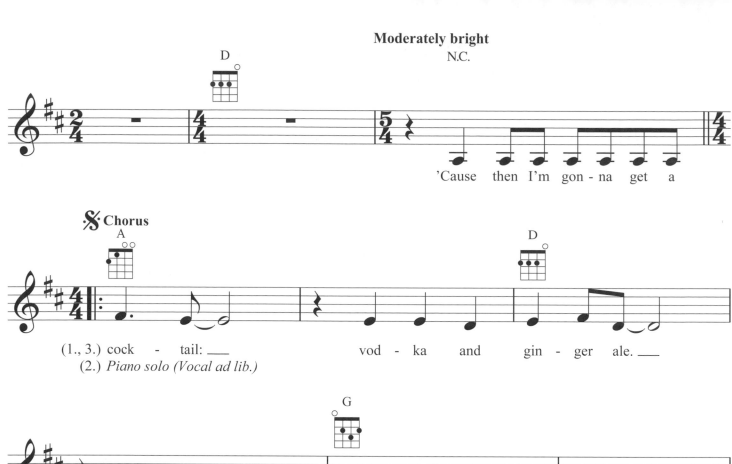

'Cause then I'm gon-na get a

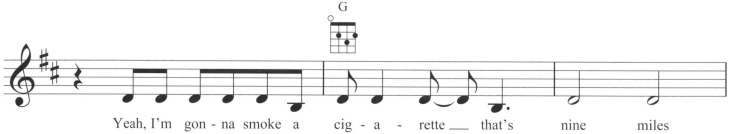

Chorus

(1., 3.) cock - tail: ___ vod - ka and gin - ger ale. ___
(2.) *Piano solo (Vocal ad lib.)*

Yeah, I'm gon - na smoke a cig - a - rette ___ that's nine miles

long. I'm gon - na kiss that pret - ty girl ___

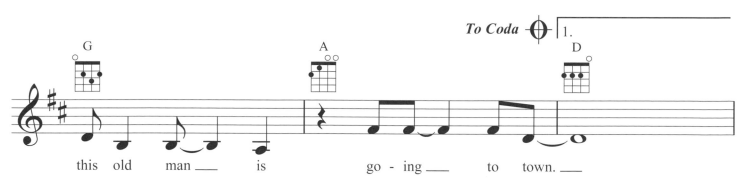

on the tilt - a - whirl. ___ Yeah,

To Coda 1.

this old man ___ is go - ing ___ to town. ___

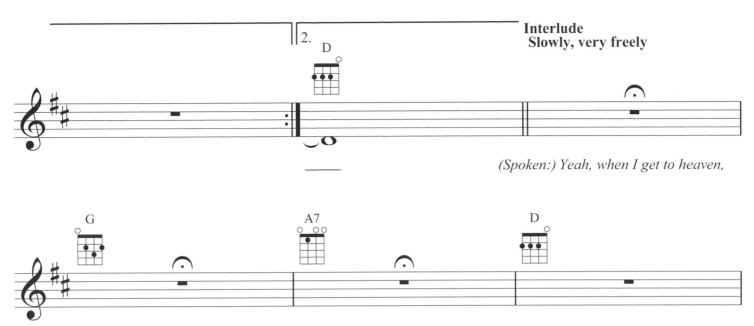

Interlude
Slowly, very freely

(Spoken:) Yeah, when I get to heaven,

I'm gonna take that wristwatch off my arm.   What are you gonna do with time after you've bought the farm?

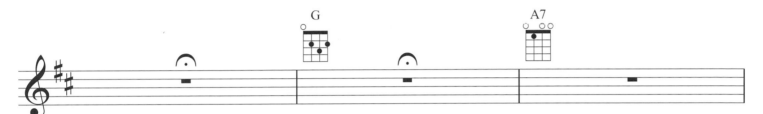

And then I'm gonna go find my mom and dad,   and good ol' brother Doug.   Why, I bet him and cousin Jackie

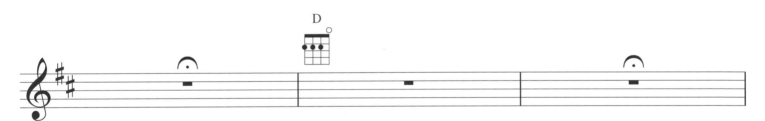

are still cutting up a rug.   Wanna see all my mama's sisters,

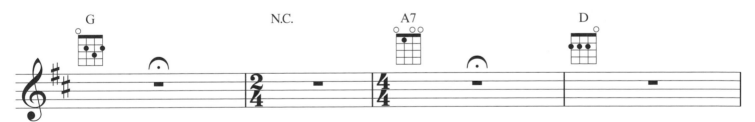

'cause that's where all the love starts.   I miss 'em all like crazy,   bless their little hearts.

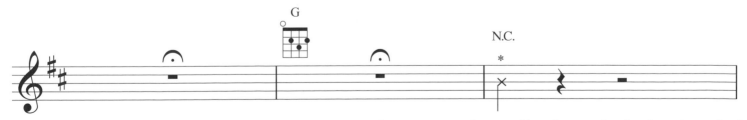

And I always will remember these words my daddy said.   He said,   "Buddy, when you're dead, you're a dead

* *Knock on ukulele.*

peckerhead."   I hope to prove him wrong.   That is . . . when I get to heaven.

Moderately bright
N.C.

D.S. al Coda

Coda

'Cause I'm gon - na have a

_____   Yeah,

Outro
G   A   D

this old man ___ is   go - ing ___ to town. ___

A

Di - dl dat - da,   doo - doot - doo, ___   dat - da,   da

D   G

doo - doot - doo, ___   doo - doo - doot - doot - doo - doot -

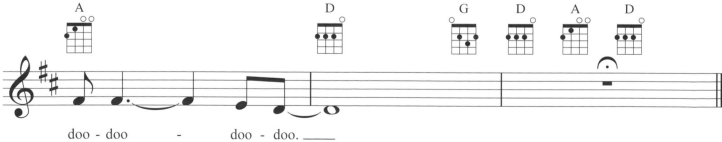

A   D   G D A D

doo - doo - doo - doo. ___

56